Human rights files, No. 23

Social security as a human right

The protection afforded
by the European Convention on Human Rights

Ana Gómez Heredero

Social Policy Department,
Directorate General of Social Cohesion
Council of Europe

Édition française :
La sécurité sociale comme droit de l'homme : la protection offerte par la Convention européenne des Droits de l'Homme
ISBN 978-92-871-6260-9

Council of Europe Publishing
F-67075 Strasbourg Cedex

ISBN 978-92-871-6261-8

Printed at the Council of Europe

Contents

Introduction

Entitlement to social security, already mentioned in the labour clauses of the Treaty of Versailles of 28 June 1919,[1] including the Constitution of the International Labour Organisation (ILO) and in the Declaration of Philadelphia of 10 May 1944, concerning the aims and objectives of the ILO, became a human right with the United Nations Universal Declaration of Human Rights of 10 December 1948 and the International Covenant on Economic, Social and Cultural Rights of 16 December 1966. The International Covenant marked an important step forward in implementation of the general principles of social security. As an international agreement (unlike the non-binding Universal Declaration), it created obligations and subjected the member states to a supervisory procedure.

In Europe the reference document in protection of human rights is the European Convention on Human Rights[2] (hereinafter "the Convention") of 4 November 1950 – one of the Council of Europe's most significant achievements. The Convention sets out a series of rights and freedoms which the member states undertake to secure to everyone within their jurisdiction.[3] It brought a further advance in effective protection of human

1. Part XIII of the Treaty of Versailles of 28 June 1919, the founding document of the International Labour Organisation (ILO).
2. The Convention for the Protection of Human Rights and Fundamental Freedoms, which was signed in Rome on 4 November 1950 and came into force on 3 September 1953.
3. Any person, having exhausted the available remedies under national law, may apply to the European Court of Human Rights on the ground of breach of the Convention.

rights by instituting supervision by a specific body, the European Court of Human Rights (hereinafter "the Court" or "the ECHR").[4]

The rights guaranteed by the Convention and the protocols to it enjoy extensive protection and, while they are essentially civil and political rights, "many of them have implications of a social and economic nature".[5] Both the Court and the European Commission of Human Rights (hereinafter "the Commission") took the view that there was "no water-tight division"[6] separating the sphere of economic and social rights from the ambit of the Convention. The Convention is thus "permeable" to social rights if it is interpreted in a dynamic and constructive manner.[7]

The European Social Charter is the Council of Europe instrument geared to guaranteeing economic and social rights. Articles 12 and 13 of the Charter cover rights in the social security and social assistance fields. The European Committee of Social Rights, which is the body responsible for interpreting the Charter, has long recognised the right to social and medical assistance (Article 13) as an individual right.[8] The supervisory mechanism of the European Social Charter is based on annual reports and a collective complaint procedure. Under the latter, the European Committee of Social Rights is responsible for deciding whether the situation in question is in breach of one or more provision(s) of the Charter. The Committee of Ministers may subsequently recommend that the state concerned take steps to bring the situation into conformity with the Charter.

The European Code of Social Security, its additional Protocol, and the Revised Code, which are the Council of Europe's basic standard-setting instruments on social security, do not create, in general, individual rights

4. Until 31 October 1998, applications were first examined by the European Commission of Human Rights before being referred, if appropriate, to the Court. On 1 November 1998, Protocol No. 11 came into force, reorganising the supervisory machinery established by the Convention. The Court, in its new single, full-time form now had direct and exclusive jurisdiction for applications by individuals alleging breach of the Convention.
5. ECHR, *Airey v. Ireland*, 9 October 1979 (Application No. 6289/73).
6. *Ibid.*
7. Working Group on Social Rights, document reference GT-DH-SOC (2005) 001.
8. G. Gori, "Domestic Enforcement of the European Social Charter: the way forward", in G. de Burca and B. de Witte, *Social Rights in Europe*, Oxford University Press, 2005, p. 83.

that can be invoked direct before the courts. They do, however, establish an international system of supervision based on national reports which produces annual resolutions of the Committee of Ministers in respect of each member state. The resolutions confirm that the contracting parties are fulfilling the obligations they have accepted or, if they are not, recommend measures they can take to rectify the situation.

While social security rights are not explicitly mentioned in the European Convention on Human Rights, they nonetheless fall within its scope.

European Court of Human Rights case-law on social security

How does the case-law of the Court protect rights in relation to social security?[9]

The first point to be made is that the Court acts in response to individual applications: "The Convention is intended to guarantee not rights that are theoretical or illusory but rights that are practical and effective."[10]

A second significant point concerns the "margin of discretion" principle, which lends itself to very loose and wide-ranging interpretation. The "margin of discretion" is based on the belief that national authorities are better placed to assess certain situations – notably their economic and social aspects. States are therefore allowed to adopt measures for the good of the national economy which may restrict guaranteed rights, always provided the principles of legality, proportionality and legitimacy of the aim pursued are not infringed.

In considering whether national authorities have exceeded the "margin of discretion", the Court takes into account the economic and

9. The term *social security* is used here in the broad sense and includes social and medical assistance.

10. ECHR, *Airey v. Ireland.* (See, *mutatis mutandis*, the judgment of 23 July 1968 in the *Belgian Linguistic case*, Series A No. 6, p. 31, §§3 *in fine* and 4; the *Golder* judgment of 21 February 1975, Series A No. 18, p. 18, §35 *in fine*; the *Luedicke, Belkacem and Koç* judgment of 28 November 1978, Series A No. 29, pp 17-18, §42; and the *Marckx* judgment of 13 June 1979, Series A No. 31, p. 15, §31.)

social context in the country concerned at the time of the disputed occurrence.[11]

The final point is that social security rights under the Convention depend crucially both on recognition of procedural guarantees and substantive protection of certain rights. Case-law has also evolved significantly in this regard. Moreover, certain provisions of the European Social Charter have been echoed in the Court's rulings, in inadmissibility decisions as well as judgments.[12]

PROTECTION OF PROCEDURAL RIGHTS IN THE FIELD OF SOCIAL SECURITY

Recognition of certain procedural guarantees with regard to rights in the field of social security has been extensively discussed by the bodies supervising the Convention. The Court's case-law has developed very significantly here.

The Convention offers procedural guarantees via the right to a fair trial as recognised in Article 6§1.

Article 6§1: Right to a fair trial

"In the determination of his civil rights and obligations ... everyone is entitled to a ... hearing within a reasonable time by [a] tribunal ..."

This provision has been applied in disputes about social security as a result of the Court's interpreting the concept of "civil rights and obligations" in a dynamic and constructive way. It has developed the concept in cases concerning both social security benefits and social contributions.

11. *Rasmussen v. Denmark*, judgment of 28 November 1984 (Application No. 8777/79).
12. *Sigurdur A. Sigurjónsson v. Iceland*, ECHR (1993), Series A, no. 254, 35; *Gustafsson v. Sweden*, ECHR (1996), Reports 1996-II for collective complaint (Article 6 of the European Social Charter); *Wilson, National Union of Journalists and others v. the United Kingdom*, Court judgment of 2 October 2002, Appl. Nos. 30668/96, 30671/96 and 30678/96., paras. 30-33 and 48, (Articles 5 and 6 ESC); *Sánchez Navajas v. Spain*, ECHR, admissibility decision, Appl. no. 57442/00, para. 2; *Koua Poirrez v. France*, Court judgment of 30 September 2003, Appl. no. 40892/98, §§29 and 39.

Cases concerning social-security benefits

Introduction

Do social security allowances fall within the scope of Article 6§1 as rights of a civil nature?

Firstly, according to the Court's case-law, the concept of "civil rights" cannot be interpreted solely by reference to the domestic law of the respondent state.[13] The "civil right" is an autonomous concept for interpretation in accordance with the Convention.[14]

How civil rights are defined in disputes about social security benefits has been a highly controversial question and one that has led to differing interpretations by the Convention bodies.

In the first cases concerning social security, the Court had to assess meticulously the public-law and private-law aspects of the rights in question to determine whether they were of a civil nature.

This is what it did in its judgments in the cases of *Feldbrugge v. the Netherlands* and *Deumeland v. the Federal Republic of Germany*, both delivered in 1986, the first concerning the right to sickness benefit and the second the right to a widow's pension.[15] The first factor identified by the Court as suggesting that the dispute fell within the sphere of public law was the character of the legislation; the second was the compulsory nature of the social security insurance schemes in question; and the third was assumption by the state, or by public or semi-public institutions, of responsibility for ensuring social protection. Among factors characteristic of the sphere of private law, on the other hand, the Court cited "the personal and economic nature" of the asserted rights, the connection between the social security scheme and the contract of employment and, finally, the affinities between social security schemes and private-sector insurance. On the basis of this analysis the Court concluded in both cases that the features of private law outweighed those of public law. The pro-

13. Judgment in *König v. the Federal Republic of Germany*, 28 June 1978, Application No. 6232/73.
14. Judgment in *Mennitto v. Italy*, 5 October 2000, Application No. 33804/96.
15. The Commission had ruled that both cases were admissible (Decision of 15 November 1983).

cedural guarantees afforded by Article 6§1 could therefore be applied to cases of this type.

Not all the judges shared these findings, however. A minority delivered a dissenting opinion that Article 6§1 was inapplicable. On the basis of the United Nations and Council of Europe preparatory work on the Convention, they held that use of the expression "civil rights and obligations" must have been intended by the drafters of the Convention to set some limit on the application of Article 6. They concluded that "there exist areas within the field of public administration subject to special institutional regimes, such as that relating to social security, under which the rights and obligations of the individual not of a private nature may justifiably, for various reasons ... be determined by special procedures of adjustment rather than by tribunals complying with all the requirements of Article 6§1".[16]

In subsequent cases the civil nature of rights in relation to social security benefits has not been questioned.[17] "Today the general rule is that Article 6§1 does apply in the field of social insurance."[18] Intervention by the state is not, of itself, sufficient to establish that Article 6§1 is inapplicable. On the contrary, in both *Salesi v. Italy* and *Schuler-Zgraggen v. Switzerland*, the justification for finding Article 6§1 applicable was that the applicants had suffered interference "with their means of subsistence" and were claiming "an individual, economic right" that flowed from specific rules – those of the Constitution in the *Salesi* case and those of a Federal statute in the case of *Schuler-Zgraggen*.

Furthermore, Article 6§1 applies irrespective of the status of the parties, the character of the legislation governing the "dispute" and the character of the authority with jurisdiction in the matter.[19]

16. Joint dissenting opinion of judges Ryssdal, Bindschedler-Robert, Lagergren, Matscher, Sir Vincent Evans, Bernhardt and Gersing.
17. Judgments in the cases of *Nibbio v. Italy*, *Borgese v. Italy*, *Biondi v. Italy*, *Monaco v. Italy* and *Lestini v. Italy*, 26 February 1992.
18. Judgments in *Salesi v. Italy*, 26 February 1993, and *Schuler-Zgraggen v. Switzerland*, 24 June 1993.
19. See judgment in *Georgiadis v. Greece*, 29 May 1997, §34 (Application No. 26643/95).

The procedural protection afforded by the Court was further extended to cover social assistance with the judgments in *Salesi v. Italy* and *Mennitto v. Italy,* cases which were concerned respectively with a social assistance benefit and an allowance for families caring at home for family members with disabilities.

For the Convention's procedural guarantees to be applicable, disputes must also concern a "right" already recognised in the domestic law of the state concerned. "The Court reiterates that, according to the principles laid down in its case-law, it must first ascertain whether there was a 'dispute' [...] over a 'right' which can be said, at least on arguable grounds, to be recognised under domestic law. The dispute must be genuine and serious; it may relate not only to the actual existence of a right but also to its scope and the manner of its exercise."[20]

Examples of applying Article 6§1

Access to an independent and impartial tribunal

Kovachev v. Bulgaria, report of the Commission, 28 October 1997 (violation)[21]

The applicant, who had a physical disability, received a pension and monthly social assistance allowances. When he applied for additional social assistance allowances he was refused them. He applied to the Court on the basis that he had been denied access to an independent and impartial tribunal to decide his case.

The Commission found in this case that Article 6 had been contravened by application of the 1992 Social Welfare Regulations, which made no provision for referral to the courts of disputes concerning social benefits, making all such disputes a matter for the administrative authorities only.

20. *Salesi v. Italy* and *Mennitto v. Italy* §23.
21. Application No. 29303/95.

Effective protection by the courts

Zednik v. the Czech Republic, judgment of 28 June 2005 (violation)[22]

The applicant had been deprived of partial invalidity benefit by the Czech social security authorities. Two courts had upheld that decision; the case then came before the Constitutional Court, which, after requiring the applicant to complete a number of formalities, ruled that the application was out of time. The applicant complained that he had been denied access to a tribunal inasmuch as the Constitutional Court's decision had been unjustified and in breach of Article 6§1.

The ECHR found that the "right to a fair trial" – of which the right of access was one aspect – was not absolute. By its nature, it required regulation on the part of the state, which had some margin of discretion in the matter. Nonetheless, limitations applied could not restrict the right in such a manner or to such an extent that its very substance was undermined.

The Court ruled that the Constitutional Court had been over-insistent on procedural formalities and that its interpretation of a procedural requirement had "prevented an examination of the merits of the applicant's case, in breach of the right to effective protection by the courts" (§33).

Length of proceedings

The criteria used to assess whether the length of proceedings is reasonable have been established by ECHR case-law and include the complexity of the case, the behaviour of the applicant and the conduct of the competent authorities. In this last regard, account is taken of the nature of the matter at stake for the applicant.[23]

22. Application No. 74328/01.

23. *Nuutinen v. Finland*, judgment of 27 June 2000, Application No. 32842/96. See also *Trikovi v. Slovenia*, No. 39914/98, 12 June 2001, §44; *Diaz Aparicio v. Spain*, No. 49468/99, 11 October 2001, §20; *H.T. v. Germany*, No. 38073/97, 11 October 2001, §31; and *Becker v. Germany*, No. 45448/99, 26 September 2002, §20, among many others.

Deumeland v. the Federal Republic of Germany, judgment of 29 May 1986 (violation)[24]

Mr Deumeland was continuing proceedings brought by his late mother, who had applied for supplementary widow's pension on the ground that her husband's death had resulted from an industrial accident. In his application, Mr Deumeland alleged that the social courts had not given the case a fair hearing within a reasonable time, contrary to the requirements of Article 6§1. The Commission concluded that Article 6§1 did not apply but the Court's finding was that Article 6§1 had been contravened.

The main issue was whether there was a causal link between the accident (which had occurred between the workplace and home) and the death. This had a crucial bearing on whether additional years' service could be awarded, increasing the value of Mrs Deumeland's old-age pension when she became a widow. The dispute had lasted almost 11 years. The case gave rise to much debate about whether the right in question was a civil right. In the end the Court ruled that Article 6§1 was applicable and that it had been contravened by failure to meet the reasonable-time requirement.

Salesi v. Italy, judgment of 26 February 1993 (violation)[25]

Ms Salesi had claimed a monthly invalidity allowance, which Latium social security services had refused her. Proceedings in the domestic courts had lasted just over six years. In her application, which the Commission ruled to be admissible, she complained of the length of the proceedings under Article 6§1. The Court held that Article 6§1 was applicable, in line with its judgments in *Feldbrugge* and *Deumeland*. It considered that the case was not a complex one and that Ms Salesi had not contributed to the delay. Thus "in view of what was at stake for the applicant", the Court ruled that the time the proceedings had taken was excessive and unreasonable.

24. Application No. 9384/81.
25. Application No. 13023/87.

Henra v. France, judgment of 29 April 1998 (violation)[26]

The applicant's father was a haemophiliac who needed frequent blood transfusions. Tests carried out on the applicant's mother at the time of her pregnancy and on his father showed that they were both HIV-positive, and when the applicant was born he was also HIV-positive. His application for compensation before the Conseil d'Etat concluded with acknowledgement of the state's liability for the infection with the virus after transfusion of untreated blood products, and the victims were awarded lump-sum compensation (§39).

Before the ECHR, the applicant complained of the length of time taken to consider his compensation claim against the state and alleged breach of Article 6§1 of the Convention.

The Court held that "what was at stake in the proceedings [...] was of crucial importance to the applicant, who has been HIV-positive since birth. In short, exceptional diligence was called for in this instance, notwithstanding the number of cases to be dealt with, in particular as the facts of the controversy had been known to the Government for several years and its seriousness must have been obvious to them" (§68).

Jacquie and Ledun v. France, judgment of 28 March 2000 (violation)[27]

The applicants – the widow and the daughter of a person who had been infected with hepatitis C – complained under Article 6§1 of the length of administrative proceedings that were still pending after more than seven years. The state had been found liable for the infection and had been ordered to pay compensation but payment had been delayed by an appeal on points of law. When the ECHR delivered its ruling, the case was still pending before the Conseil d'Etat.

The Court noted that the length of time the proceedings had taken was mainly the result of the conduct of the authorities and administrative courts. It asserted that it was the responsibility of the contracting states to organise their legal systems in such a way that their courts could guarantee the right to a final decision within a reasonable time. Taking into account

26. Application No. 110/1997/894/1106.
27. Application No. 40493/98.

the conduct of the competent authorities and the nature of what was at stake for the applicants, the Court ruled that the seven years which the proceedings had already lasted could not be considered a reasonable period of time (§23).

Mennitto v. Italy, judgment of 5 October 2000 (violation)

The local public health service had not followed up Mr Mennitto's application for the allowance available in Italian law to families caring at home for family members with disabilities. He had therefore taken proceedings against the health service in the administrative court. Before the ECHR he maintained that the length of the proceedings in the administrative court infringed Article 6§1.

The regional administrative court had, however, dismissed his claim on the ground that it was based not on a right but on legitimate interest.

The ECHR held that the right in question was an economic one and a "civil right" within the meaning of its case-law, and that the requirements of Article 6§1 thus applied. The Court did not examine whether the concept of a "right" within the meaning of Article 6§1 covered only a personal entitlement or took in legitimate interest. After examining the facts, and in view of previous findings against Italy in the matter, the Court held that the length of the proceedings had had a decisive effect on the applicant's civil rights and did not meet the "reasonable time" requirement (§27).

Kritt v. France, judgment of 19 March 2002 (violation)[28]

Ms Kritt had been infected with hepatitis C and Aids during transfusion of blood products. The applicants (Ms Kritt and her father, mother and brother) claimed compensation from the Paris hospital authority (*Assistance publique – Hôpitaux de Paris*) for injury caused by the double infection. They argued that in French case-law blood-transfusion centres were liable, even in the absence of fault, for injury caused by substandard products supplied by them (§12). Before the Court, the applicants claimed that the obstacles they had encountered and the delay in the compensation proceedings contravened Article 6§1.

28. Application No. 57753/00.

The Court noted that, at the date of its ruling, almost four years had passed since the application for compensation had been made and that the case was still pending in the Paris administrative court. It pointed out the significance of the proceedings for the applicant and ruled that "exceptional diligence is required from the authorities when an applicant is suffering from an incurable disease and has a reduced life expectancy" (§14).

Mocie v. France, judgment of 8 April 2003 (violation)[29]

Mr Mocie was drawing benefit for 90% invalidity. He submitted a number of appeals to the administrative courts claiming a special allowance for people with major disabilities and an attendance allowance. He was awarded the special allowance but it had not yet been paid to him when he applied to the ECHR, by which time the administrative proceedings had taken more than 14 years. His second claim had been rejected after almost eight years of administrative proceedings.

The Court noted that the applicant's invalidity benefit constituted virtually his entire resources. The proceedings were therefore of great importance to him, thus warranting particular diligence on the part of the authorities. Finding that the conduct of the administrative and judicial authorities was open to criticism, it concluded that Article 6§1 had been infringed in both cases.

Failure to enforce a judgment or administrative decision at national level

Burdov v. Russia, judgment of 7 May 2002 (violation)[30]

Following the Chernobyl disaster, Mr Burdov was called up by the military authorities to take part in emergency operations on the site of the nuclear plant. He subsequently experienced health problems caused by having been exposed to radioactivity. He was awarded compensation, then the amount was reduced and the payment was not actually made, due to lack of funds. The applicant alleged that the failure to enforce the

29. Application No. 46096/99.
30. Application No. 59498/00.

final judgment in his favour was incompatible with the Convention. He cited Article 6§1 and Article 1 of Protocol No. 1.

The Court held that "it is not open to a state authority to cite lack of funds as an excuse for not honouring a judgment debt. In the instant case, the applicant should not have been prevented from benefiting from the success of the litigation ... on the ground of alleged financial difficulties experienced by the state (§35)". It concluded that "by failing for years to take the necessary measures to comply with the final judicial decisions in the present case, the Russian authorities deprived the provisions of Article 6§1 of all useful effect" (§37).

Makarova and others v. Russia, judgment of 24 February 2005 (violation)[31]

The applicants, Russian nationals, had applied to the Russian courts for social welfare benefits or an increase in the amount of pension paid to them by the social welfare office. They complained that failure to enforce judgments in their favour delivered by the Russian courts had infringed their right of access to a court and their right to the peaceful enjoyment of their possessions (Article 6§1 of the Convention and Article 1 of Protocol No. 1).

The Court referred to its previous case-law (see the *Burdov* judgment, §35) and ruled that lack of funds could not justify non-payment of the sums awarded (§32). It concluded that, by failing for such a long period of time to take the necessary measures to comply with the judicial decisions in the case, the Russian authorities had deprived the provisions of Article 6§1 of all useful effect and violated Article 1 of Protocol No. 1 to the Convention.

31. Application No. 67099/01. See also: *Sharenok v. Ukraine* of 22 February 2005, concerning non-payment of the debts of the applicant's former employer, a publicly owned company; and *Plotnikovy v. Russia* and *Poznakhirina v. Russia* of 24 February 2005, concerning non-payment of social welfare benefits awarded by the Russian courts.

Cases concerning payment of social contributions

Introduction

The Court has also been called upon to determine cases concerning the applicability of Article 6§1 in disputes about the contributions provided for under social security schemes. The reasoning it followed in relation to the right to benefit was not automatically applicable in these cases.

Its judgment of 9 December 1994 in the case of *Schouten and Meldrum v. the Netherlands*[32] supplemented the Article 6§1 definition of "civil rights and obligations".

There had been a dispute between two physiotherapists and the professional association responsible in the Netherlands for managing sickness insurance, unemployment insurance and invalidity insurance for people working in that field. The association billed the applicants for contributions on the basis that they were not independent practitioners but employees, that is to say persons bound by a contract of employment or the "social equivalent" of such a contract. The practitioners then asked the association for written confirmation of its decision, with the reasoning behind it, this being a prerequisite for taking the matter to court. The association took more than 19 months to reply in the case of Mr Schouten and 17 months in the case of Mr Meldrum. The applicants alleged that Article 6§1 of the Convention had been breached because their cases had not been dealt with in a reasonable time and they had thus been denied a fair trial.

The Government of the Netherlands counterargued that the dispute concerned not social security benefits but contributions, which were akin to taxation and therefore did not fall within the definition of "civil rights and obligations".

In its judgment, the Court stated that it was not sufficient to show that a dispute was "pecuniary" in nature for Article 6 to be applicable. There might exist "pecuniary" obligations *vis-à-vis* the state that were exclusively in the public realm.

32. Applications Nos. 19005/91 and 19006/91.

The Court adopted the same approach as in the disputes about social security benefits. It noted that the "civil" nature of rights and obligations was an autonomous concept and it analysed the various relevant features of public and private law in determining whether the contested "obligation" could be regarded as a "civil" one. It concluded that the private-law features outweighed the public-law ones, particularly in relation to the connection between payment of contributions and the employment contract. It also drew an analogy between social security schemes and private insurance schemes. It held that the contributions demanded fell within the definition of "civil rights and obligations" and concluded that Article 6§1 was applicable.

In subsequent cases the question as to whether disputes about social contributions fell within the scope of Article 6 has ceased to be asked – see *Perhirin and 29 others v. France*, judgment of 14 May 2002; *M.B. v. France*, judgment of 13 September 2005; and *Diaz Ochoa v. Spain*, judgment of 22 June 2006.

Examples of applying Article 6§1

Length of proceedings

Perhirin and 29 others v. France, judgment of 14 May 2002 (violation)[33]

The applicants in this case had challenged the basis used for assessing their contributions to the welfare scheme for agricultural self-employed workers. They claimed that it was too high and complained that there was no weighting device for taking their actual circumstances into account.

Before the Court they complained that the excessive length of the two sets of administrative proceedings contravened their right to have their case heard within a reasonable time.

The Court ruled that the length of the proceedings was essentially attributable to the judicial authorities and that there had therefore been a violation of Article 6§1.

33. Application No. 14518/89

Fairness of proceedings

M.B. v. France, judgment of 13 September 2005 (violation)[34]

The applicant had been laid off and awarded a redundancy payment. After the Court of Cassation rejected two further claims by him – for employer's pension contributions and a supplementary redundancy payment – he applied to the ECHR on the ground of unfairness of the proceedings.

The Court concluded that Article 6§1 had been infringed in that in the Court of Cassation the reporting judge's report, which had been available to the Advocate General, had not been disclosed to the applicant beforehand, making it impossible for him to respond to the Advocate General's submissions (§22).

Right to a court hearing

Diaz Ochoa v. Spain, judgment of 22 June 2006 (violation) [35]

The applicant, who had been the managing director of the Plasti-Rec company, lost his job in 1988. He handed over to his partner, J.M.M., who ran the company until it closed in 1989.

In 1991, J.M.M. lodged a claim against the National Social Security Institute (INSS) and against the firm of Diaz Ochoa, trading as Plasti-Rec, seeking a change in the calculation basis for his invalidity benefit. Judgment was given partially in J.M.M.'s favour and in the absence of the co-defendant, Mr Diaz Ochoa. In execution of the judgment, the INSS applied to recover from the applicant's earnings the amounts due in social security contributions. Mr Diaz Ochoa did not become aware of the proceedings against him until October 1998. He made a number of applications to the courts, which were rejected. Before the ECHR, he complained under Article 6§1 that as co-defendant he had not been informed of the proceedings against him.

The Court held that the particular combination of circumstances in the case had had the effect of depriving him of proper access to a court, thus

34. Application No. 65935/01
35. Application No. 423/03

preventing him from contesting the case. The applicant's right to a court had thus been infringed in its very essence (§50).

Protection of substantive rights in the social-security field

Substantive protection of rights is highly complex because in this area states enjoy some discretion and there is a risk of imposing obligations on them that they did not commit themselves to. At the same time the law evolves and care must be taken that the Convention continues to be a dynamic instrument, interpreted in the light of present-day conditions. In line with this progressive approach the Court may impose positive obligations, some of them of a financial nature. "The Court is aware that the further realisation of social and economic rights is largely dependent on the situation – notably financial – reigning in the state in question. On the other hand, the Convention must be interpreted in the light of present-day conditions."[36]

In this way, the Court reflects through its case-law the evolution of concerns about social protection within the member states. In particular, recognition of the pecuniary nature of certain social rights means they can be regarded as falling within the scope of Article 1 of Protocol No. 1.

Similarly, the Court's interpretation of Article 14 of the Convention has enabled it to engage with unequal treatment as regards award of social benefits or advantages.

The Court's judgments also reflect a trend towards improved protection for people living in destitution, poverty or social exclusion.[37]

---

36. Judgment in the *Marckx* case of 13 June 1979. See also *Airey v. Ireland*, judgment of 9 October 1979 (Application No. 6289/73).
37. According to the Working Group on Social Rights (GT-DH-SOC), "The prospect of case-law developing further in this direction seems to reflect the principle of respect for human dignity and the concerns expressed in Recommendation R (2000) 3 of the Committee of Ministers of the Council of Europe". Recommendation R (2000) 3, on the right to satisfaction of basic material needs of persons in situations of extreme hardship, was adopted by the Committee of Ministers on 19 January 2000, at the 694th meeting of the Ministers' Deputies.

Articles 2, 3 and 8 of the Convention may be applicable to some such situations.

Article 1 of Protocol No. 1 (Protection of property)

"Every natural or legal person is entitled to the peaceful enjoyment of his possessions. No one shall be deprived of his possessions except in the public interest and subject to the conditions provided for by law and by the general principles of international law.

The preceding provisions shall not, however, in any way impair the right of a state to enforce such laws as it deems necessary to control the use of property in the general interest or to secure the payment of taxes or other contributions or penalties."

This article substantively guarantees the right to property and contains three distinct principles: the first, of a general nature, is that of respect for property, enunciated in the first sentence of the first paragraph; the second, in the following sentence, lays down specific conditions on which people may be deprived of property; and the third, in the second paragraph, recognises that states have a right, for certain purposes, to control the use of property.

The right to social benefit and social assistance does not derive directly from the Convention. The Commission, for example, rejected a number of applications concerning the award of non-contributory benefits. These included non-contributory allowances for invalidity, old age and widowhood, as well as unemployment and family benefits, sickness benefit and housing benefit.[38]

A different view was taken in cases concerning contributory pensions or allowances. Here the Commission stated that the duty to contribute to a social security scheme might, in certain circumstances, give rise to a

38. See, for example, Applications Nos. 92/55 v. Belgium (pensions), decision of 16 December 1955, *Yearbook* I, p. 1990; No. 2114/64 v. the Federal Republic of Germany (pension), decision of 17 December 1966, *Collection of Decisions* No. 23, p. 10; No. 2374/64 v. Norway and Denmark (sickness), decision of 15 December 1967 (unpublished); No. 2380/64 v. Federal Republic of Germany (old age), decision of 7 February 1967 (unpublished).

property right over certain assets thus constituted and that the existence of such a right might depend on the way in which these assets were used for the payment of a pension.[39] In the case of an individual who had contributed to a social security scheme creating entitlement to benefit, it thus interpreted the right to those benefits as a property right within the meaning of Article 1 of Protocol No. 1.

This strand of case-law has developed further, albeit not entirely unambiguously, in extending the scope of protection. Many of the cases concerned relate to discrimination in access to benefit.

Article 1 of Protocol No. 1 becomes applicable if the individual concerned has contributed to a fund created by the state for the purpose of paying pensions or allowances at a later date. Such contributions are required under the right of the state "to secure the payment of taxes or other contributions or penalties" (ECHR, *Van Raalte v. the Netherlands*, judgment of 21 February 1997).

Both the contributions to these funds and the benefits paid from them fall within the scope of Article 1 of Protocol No. 1. In the case of *Gaygusuz v. Austria*[40] the Court held that entitlement to benefit was linked to the payment of contributions and that a person who had paid his or her contributions could not be refused the benefit in question. "Entitlement to this social benefit is therefore linked to the payment of contributions to the unemployment insurance fund, which is a precondition for the payment of unemployment benefit … It follows that there is no entitlement to emergency assistance where such contributions have not been made."

In the same judgment, the Court went further again, defining the right to emergency assistance, granted by the state to persons in need, as a pecuniary right: "… the right to emergency assistance – in so far as provided for in the applicable legislation – is a pecuniary right for the purposes of Article 1 of Protocol No. 1. That provision is therefore applicable without it being necessary to rely solely on the link between entitlement

39. *Müller v. Austria*, decision of 16 December 1974
40. Judgment of 16 September 1996

to emergency assistance and the obligation to pay "taxes or other contributions"."

Moreover, a "claim" may constitute a "possession" within the meaning of Article 1 of Protocol No. 1, provided that it is sufficiently well established to be enforceable. Such was the case, for example, with an arbitration award which clearly recognised the state's liability up to a maximum of specified amounts.[41]

Ruling in the case of *Wessels-Bergervoet v. the Netherlands* on 4 June 2002, the Court confirmed that "the applicant's rights to a pension under the General Old Age Pensions Act could be regarded as a 'possession' within the meaning of Article 1 of Protocol No. 1".

In the case of *Willis v. United Kingdom* (judgment of 11 June 2002), the Court did not address the question of whether "a social security benefit must be contributory in nature in order for it to constitute a 'possession' for the purposes of Article 1 of Protocol No. 1". It took the view that entitlement to a lump-sum widow's payment and to widow's allowance – in so far as provided for in the applicable legislation – constituted a sufficiently pecuniary right to fall within the ambit of Article 1 of Protocol No. 1.

In its judgment in the case of *Azinas v. Cyprus* on 20 June 2002, the Court confirmed that, while the right to a pension was not, as such, guaranteed by the Convention, "according to the case-law of the Convention institutions, the right to a pension which is based on employment can in certain circumstances be assimilated to a property right". That applies, for example, when special contributions have been paid,[42] and indeed the Court had already gone a step further in its interpretation: "This may be the case where [...] the employer, as in the present case, has given a more general undertaking to pay a pension on conditions which can be considered to be part of the employment contract."[43]

41. See judgment in *Stran Greek Refineries and Stratis Andreadis v. Greece*, 9 December 1994, §61.
42. Judgment in *Gaygusuz v. Austria*
43. *Sture Stigson v. Sweden*, No. 12264/86, Commission decision of 13 July 1988, Decisions and Reports 57, p. 131

The *Azinas* finding quoted was in a chamber judgment, and the application was subsequently declared inadmissible by the Grand Chamber on the ground that available domestic remedies had not been exhausted.[44]

The chamber reasoning in *Azinas* was followed in the *Buche* and *Koua Poirrez* judgments.

The Court's rulings on the applicability of Article 1 of Protocol No. 1 have none the less been ambivalent, particularly in relation to non-contributory benefits. As in its deliberations about the concept of "civil rights and obligations", differing views are to be found concerning interpretation of the concepts of "possessions" and "property".

This was what, in 2004, led Section IV of the Court to relinquish jurisdiction in the *Stec and others v. the United Kingdom* case to the Grand Chamber.

The applicants in the case complained of sex discrimination in relation to the award of "reduced earnings allowance" and/or "retirement allowance" – which are non-contributory benefits. They alleged there had been a violation of Article 14 in conjunction with Article 1 of Protocol No. 1. Because, however, Article 14 has no independent existence, the Court had to begin by considering whether Article 1 of Protocol No. 1 was applicable.

The Grand Chamber declared the application to be admissible. It asserted that "if [...] a contracting state has in force legislation providing for the payment as of right of a welfare benefit – whether conditional or not on the prior payment of contributions – that legislation must be regarded as generating a proprietary interest falling within the ambit of Article 1 of Protocol No. 1 for persons satisfying its requirements" (decision of 6 July 2005, §54).

A "proprietary interest" thus falls within interpretation of the concept of "possessions".

The Court ruled, however, that Article 14 had not been violated. In a concurring opinion,[45] one of the judges stated that he had voted with the majority of the Grand Chamber not on the issue of non-violation but on

44. Grand Chamber judgment in *Azinas v. Cyprus*, 28 April 2004, §§40-42
45. Concurring opinion of Judge Borrego Borrego.

the basis that the applicants "could not be considered to have 'possessions' within the meaning of Article 1 of Protocol No. 1, which guarantees the protection of property". This opinion illustrates that the scope of the concept of "possessions" remains a controversial question in 2006.

Examples of applying Article 1 of Protocol No. 1

Federspev v. Italy, decision of 6 September 1995 (inadmissible)[46]

The applicants in this case complained that the state had not provided any mechanism for automatic adjustment of pensions, and an adjustment for which there was legal provision had been deferred on two occasions. Because the pensions paid to the applicants were inadequate in relation to the cost of living, Article 1 of Protocol No. 1 had allegedly been violated.

The Commission accepted that the individual's right to be covered by an old-age pension system to which he or she had contributed came within the ambit of protection of the right to property. It none the less found that "Article 1 of Protocol No. 1 could not be interpreted as bestowing a right to an income of a particular level". The applicants benefited from an old-age pension system to which they had contributed, and the lack of a system for adjusting pensions and the deferral of indexing could not be interpreted as infringing their pecuniary rights since the substance of those rights had not been affected.

Larioshina v. Russia, decision of 23 April 2002 (inadmissible)[47]

The applicant claimed that the amount of old-age pension and other social payments that she received from the social security authorities had not been properly calculated and that the amount was insufficient for her to live on. She contended that the failure of the domestic courts to recognise her property claims and award damages against the social security authorities interfered with her "possessions" – the right to which was guaranteed under Article 1 of Protocol No. 1.

The Court observed that the applicant was in receipt of old-age pension and other benefits and that she had not exercised her right to apply

46. Application No. 22867/93.
47. Application No. 56679/00

for additional social benefit. It pointed out that it could not substitute itself for the national authorities, who alone were empowered to review the level of financial benefits awarded under a social assistance scheme and it concluded that there had been no interference with the applicant's right to the social benefits in question.

Burdov v. Russia, judgment of 7 May 2002 (violation)[48]

The applicant in this case likewise relied on the right to property.

The Court noted that "the Shakhty City Court's decisions [...] provided the applicant with enforceable claims and not simply a general right to receive support from the state" (§40). The decisions had become final as no ordinary appeal lay against them, and enforcement proceedings had been instituted. "By failing to comply with the judgments of the Shakhty City Court, the national authorities prevented the applicant from receiving the money he could reasonably have expected to receive. The Government has not advanced any justification for this interference and the Court considers that a lack of funds cannot justify such an omission" (§41).

Azinas v. Cyprus, judgment of 20 June 2002 (violation)[49]

The applicant in this case was a former senior public official who had been stripped of pension rights following a criminal conviction.

He argued that the contributions he had paid during his 20 years' service and his employer's undertaking to finance a pension, together with his benefits and pension amount, constituted possessions for the purposes of Article 1 of Protocol No. 1 and he therefore alleged that this provision had been violated (§34).

The Court noted that the applicant, when entering the public service in Cyprus, had acquired a right which constituted a "possession" within the meaning of Article 1 of Protocol No. 1. This conclusion was reinforced by the revised version of section 79 (7) of the Public Service Law No. 33/67, providing that a pension would be paid to the wife and children of a dismissed public servant as though he had died on the date of his dismissal.

48. Application No. 59498/00; see also pp. 17 and 57.

49. Application No. 9384/81.

Ouzounis and 33 others v. Greece, judgment of 18 April 2002 (violation)[50]

The applicants complained of the refusal by the competent authorities to increase their pensions, in infringement, they maintained, of their right to enjoyment of their property under Article 1 of Protocol No. 1.

The Athens Administrative Appeal Court had ruled that the applicants were not entitled to have their pensions increased. Consequently the ECHR decided that they had never had an established claim against the Greek state. So long as the case was pending in the Greek courts, their action to obtain a pension gave rise not to a claim on which they could rely in law, but merely to the possibility of having such a claim. The Appeal Court ruling which had finally dismissed their application could not therefore have had the effect of depriving them of a possession.

Solodyuk v. Russia, judgment of 3 June 2004 (violation)[51]

Mr and Mrs Solodyuk complained that between June and December 1997, then again between January and April 1999, they had received their old-age pensions several months late and that, as a result of inflation and the devaluation of the Russian rouble during that period, their pensions had lost a significant part of their value by the time they were paid. The applicants alleged breach of Article 1 of Protocol No. 1 and of Article 6 of the Convention.

The Court observed that the delays in payment of the applicants' old-age pensions, supposedly their sole or main income, lasted continuously for over a year, involving, in many cases, three months' delay or more. The effects of very high inflation on the applicants' late pension payments at the time were such that the pensions fell significantly in value. The delay thus imposed an individual and excessive burden on the applicants. It followed that there had been a breach of Article 1 of Protocol No. 1.

50. Application No. 49144/99.
51. Application No. 9384/81.

Kjartan Ásmundsson v. Iceland, judgment of 12 October 2004 (violation)[52]

The applicant in this case was one of 54 people who had ceased to receive a disability pension following the entry into force of new legislation in relation to the award of such benefits.

The Court said that legitimate concerns about the need to resolve the pension fund's financial difficulties seemed hard to reconcile with the fact that, after the legislation came into force, the vast majority of the 689 disability pensioners continued to receive disability benefits at the same level as before, whereas only a small minority of disability pensioners had to bear the most drastic measure of all, namely the total loss of their pension entitlements. It found that the applicant was made to bear an excessive and disproportionate burden which could not be justified by the legitimate community interests relied on by the authorities. It would have been otherwise had the applicant been obliged to endure a reasonable and commensurate reduction rather than the total deprivation of his entitlements.

Article 14 (Prohibition of discrimination)

"The enjoyment of the rights and freedoms set forth in this Convention shall be secured without discrimination on any ground such as sex, race, colour, language, religion, political or other opinion, national or social origin, association with a national minority, property, birth or other status."

Article 14 has no independent existence; it constitutes one particular ingredient (non-discrimination) of each of the rights safeguarded by the Convention (see, *inter alia*, the *Marckx* judgment of 13 June 1979, §32). The articles enshrining those rights may be contravened on their own or in conjunction with Article 14. If the Court does not find a separate breach of one of those articles invoked both on its own and together with Article 14 it must also examine the case under the latter provision. On the other hand, such an examination is not generally required when the Court

52. Application No. 60669/00.

finds a violation of one of those articles taken on its own. The position is otherwise if a clear inequality of treatment in the enjoyment of the right in question is a fundamental aspect of the case.[53]

According to the Court's case-law, a distinction is discriminatory within the meaning of Article 14 if there is no "objective and reasonable justification" for it, in other words if it does not pursue a "legitimate aim" or if there is not a "reasonable relationship of proportionality between the means employed and the aim sought to be realised". In addition, the contracting states enjoy "a certain margin of appreciation … in assessing whether and to what extent differences in otherwise similar situations justify a different treatment in law".[54]

As we shall see below, the principle of non-discrimination in the enjoyment of a social right has been established by the case-law of the Court.

Examples of applying Article 14

Discrimination on the ground of sex

Article 14 of the Convention in conjunction with Article 12 (right to marry)

Rita Cannatella v. Switzerland, decision of 11 April 1996 (inadmissible)[55]

The applicant, who resided in Switzerland and suffered from a skin disease, was forbidden by the Swiss National Insurance Fund to perform any work that brought her into contact with nickel. After her employer terminated her employment contract, she received compensatory benefit for change of employment. When she became pregnant and declared her intention to stop seeking work, the Fund refused to pay her benefit. Relying on Article 12 in conjunction with Article 14 of the Convention, the applicant alleged, firstly, that her right to found a family had been violated and, secondly, that she was a victim of discrimination against women inasmuch as only women could be deprived of benefit on grounds of pregnancy.

53. Judgment in the case of *Airey v. Ireland*, 9 October 1979
54. *Buche v. the Czech Republic*, 26 November 2002
55. Application No. 25928/94.

The Commission stated in its decision that "the Convention guaranteed no right to assistance from the state to maintain a certain standard of living" and that "Article 12 did not require states parties to support financially a parent who voluntarily gave up paid work for family reasons". The Court therefore rejected the application, deeming it incompatible *ratione materiae* with the provisions of the Convention.

Article 14 of the Convention in conjunction with Article 1 of Protocol No. 1

Van Raalte v. the Netherlands,[56] *judgment of 21 February 1997 (violation)*

The complaint in this case concerned unequal treatment of men and women in relation to contributions to the social security scheme established under the General Child Care Benefits Act. Unmarried, childless men aged 45 and over were required to pay these contributions whereas women in the same circumstances were exempt.

The Court criticised this situation, which had pertained in the Netherlands prior to 1989, taking the view that there was no objective and reasonable justification for the difference in treatment. It concluded that there had been a violation of Article 14 in conjunction with Article 1 of Protocol No. 1.

Michael Matthews v. the United Kingdom, decision of 28 November 2000 (admissible)[57]

The applicant, who was aged 64 in 1997, complained of the local authorities' refusal to grant him a bus pass because he had not reached the age of 65, whereas women could obtain the free-travel pass once they reached 60 years of age.

The application was declared admissible in view of the complex issues that it raised under Article 14 of the Convention in conjunction with Article 1 of Protocol No. 1 (discrimination on the ground of sex in relation to the right to protection of property). The Court never ruled on the substance of the case, however, because the parties reached an amicable settlement.

56. Application No. 20060/92.
57. Application No. 40302/98.

Wessels-Bergervoet v. the Netherlands, judgment of 4 June 2002 (violation)[58]

The old-age pension of the applicant and her husband had been reduced by 38% because the husband had not been insured in the Netherlands for a period of 19 years when he had been working in Germany. The applicant complained that determination of the period of her social cover depended on the duration of her husband's social cover. She alleged an infringement of Article 14 of the Convention in conjunction with Article 1 of Protocol No. 1 for reasons of discrimination on the ground of sex (§37).

The Court concluded that the reduction applied to the applicant's pension had been based solely on the fact of her being married. Although the relevant legislation in the Netherlands had been changed in 1985 to give married women independent status in respect of social benefits, the Court condemned the discriminatory effect of the former legal rules. It considered that the applicant had suffered a difference of treatment that was not based on any "objective and reasonable justification". There had thus been a violation of Article 14 of the Convention in conjunction with Article 1 of Protocol No. 1 (§§53-54).

Willis v. the United Kingdom, judgment of 11 June 2002 (violation)[59]

Mr Willis was the administrator of his late wife's estate. She had been the family's primary breadwinner and had paid full social security contributions as an employed worker. Following his wife's death, the applicant stopped working in order to care full time for his children. He applied for benefits equivalent to those to which a widow whose husband had died in similar circumstances to those of Mrs Willis would have been entitled. Before the Court the applicant complained that the United Kingdom authorities' refusal to pay him the social security benefits to which he would have been entitled had he been a woman in a similar situation constituted

58. Application No. 34462/97.

59. Application No. 36042/97. See also the cases of *Cornwell v. the United Kingdom* and *Leary v. the United Kingdom*, in which judgment was delivered on 25 April 2000: the applicants in these cases complained that there was No. provision in United Kingdom law for social benefits to be payable to widowers caring for their children. The two cases concluded with an amicable settlement.

discrimination against him on the ground of sex in violation of Article 14 in conjunction with Article 1 of Protocol No. 1.

The Court noted that the applicant met the various legal criteria for award of the benefits in question and that the authorities had denied him financial benefit on the sole ground that he was a man. It ruled that there had been a violation of Article 14 in conjunction with Article 1 of Protocol No. 1.

Stec and others v. the United Kingdom [GC], judgment of 12 April 2006 (admissible)

This case originated in two applications.[60] The chamber to which they were initially assigned decided to join them and relinquish jurisdiction to the Grand Chamber.[61]

The applicants, all British nationals, complained of discrimination on the ground of sex in relation to the award of reduced-earnings allowance (REA) and retirement allowance. These earnings-related benefits are payable to employees or former employees who have suffered an accident at work or an occupational disease, with the purpose of compensating for an impairment in earning capacity. Until 1986, recipients of the REA continued to receive the allowance in addition to their old-age pension. After that date a series of legislative measures sought to remove or reduce it for claimants no longer of working age. Removal or reduction of the benefit was to take effect from pensionable age, that is 65 for men and 60 for women. Before the Court, the applicants complained of discrimination on the ground of sex as a consequence of the legislative changes that linked eligibility for REA to the pension system.

The Court concluded that there had been no violation of Article 14 of the Convention in conjunction with Article 1 of Protocol No. 1. It recognised "that the difference in state pensionable age between men and women in the United Kingdom was originally intended to correct the disadvantaged economic position of women. It continued to be reasonably and objectively justified". The United Kingdom Government's decisions as

60. Applications Nos. 65731/01 and 65900/01.

61. Article 30 of the Convention.

to the precise timing and means of putting right the inequality were not so manifestly unreasonable as to exceed its margin of appreciation. The decision to link eligibility for REA to the pension system was reasonably and objectively justified given that REA was intended to compensate for reduced earning capacity during a person's working life.

Article 14 in conjunction with Article 6§1

Schuler-Zgraggen v. Switzerland, judgment of 24 June 1993 (violation)[62]

Between 1979 and 1986, the applicant had received an allowance on the grounds of incapacity for work due to illness. From 1986, the Invalidity Insurance Board decided to discontinue the allowance on the ground that, with the birth of her child, the applicant's health had improved and she was able to look after her home and her child. Mrs Schuler-Zgraggen contested the decision in the Federal Insurance Court, which undertook to consider to what extent she was restricted in her activities as a mother and housewife but refused to assess whether she was fit to work in her previous employment, taking the view that she would have given up paid work even if her health had not been impaired. The Federal Insurance Court justified its decision on the observation "based on experience of everyday life" that many married women gave up their jobs when their first child was born and did not resume them until later.

The ECHR considered that this assumption had been decisive in the court's decision, and introduced a difference of treatment based solely on the ground of sex, for which there was no objective and reasonable justification. It concluded that there had been a violation of Article 14 of the Convention in conjunction with Article 6§1.

Discrimination on the ground of nationality

Article 14 of the Convention in conjunction with Article 1 of Protocol No. 1

Gaygusuz v. Austria, judgment of 16 September 1996 (violation)[63]

The applicant, a Turkish national who had for many years lived and worked legally in Austria, was refused an emergency allowance by the

62. Application No. 14518/89.
63. Case No. 39/1995/545/631.

employment agency because, under Austrian unemployment legislation, this type of allowance was payable only to Austrian nationals. He claimed he was a victim of discrimination against a migrant worker on the ground of nationality (§33).

The Court noted that entitlement to this social benefit was linked to payment of contributions to the unemployment insurance fund, a condition the applicant fulfilled (§39). It considered that the right to emergency assistance was a pecuniary right for the purposes of Article 1 of Protocol No. 1 (§41) and that the distinction made between Austrian nationals and non-nationals was not based on any "objective and reasonable justification" (§50).

Koua Poirrez v. France, judgment of 30 September 2003 (violation)[64]

Mr Koua Poirrez, an Ivory Coast national living in France, was registered with the Seine-Saint-Denis Occupational Counselling and Rehabilitation Board (COTOREP) as 80% disabled. The Family Allowances Office refused him an allowance for disabled adults on the grounds that he was not a French national and there was no relevant reciprocity agreement between France and Ivory Coast. The applicant complained that this was a contravention of Article 14 of the Convention in conjunction with Article 1 of Protocol No. 1.

Before the Court had ruled on the merits of the case an act was passed, on 11 May 1998, abolishing the nationality requirement for award of the benefit – which the applicant immediately received. The Court nevertheless delivered a ruling concerning the period preceding the act, and applied to the allowance for disabled adults the principle that a non-contributory benefit constituted property (§37). Prior to 1998 the applicant had satisfied all the other conditions of entitlement to the benefit. Even though France had not been bound by a reciprocity agreement at the time, in ratifying the Convention it had made a commitment to secure the Convention rights to everyone within its jurisdiction. Accordingly there

64. Application No. 40892/98.

had been a violation of Article 14 of the Convention in conjunction with Article 1 of Protocol No. 1.

Discrimination in relation to other categories of people

Buche v. the Czech Republic, judgment of 26 November 2002 (violation)[65]

This application concerned the discriminatory suspension, under legislation passed in 1993, of payment of an army pension. The applicant had earned entitlement to the benefit on the basis of his former employment as a judge in the military court service; it had been discontinued as a consequence of his transfer (as a judge) to the ordinary courts. The applicant contended that his right to enjoyment of his property had been infringed and that he had been discriminated against in comparison with other former army personnel who received the benefit.

The Court considered that there was, undeniably, a difference in the treatment applied to different categories of former army personnel with regard to payment of their pension. Even taking account of the margin of discretion which states enjoyed in controlling the use of property, the Government had not justified the distinction. The Court held that there was no objective and reasonable justification for such a distinction and that there had, therefore, been a violation of Article 14 in conjunction with Article 1 of Protocol No. 1.

Article 2 (The right to life)

"Everyone's right to life shall be protected by law."

Introduction

Article 2, wording thus what is a basic value of democratic societies, is one of the Convention's most important articles, placing a duty on states to take appropriate steps to safeguard the lives of those within its jurisdiction.[66]

65. Application No. 36541/97
66. *L.C.B v. the United Kingdom*, judgment of 9 June 1998

Examples of applying Article 2

La Parola and others v. Italy, decision of 30 November 2000 (inadmissible)[67]

The applicants in this case were three Italian nationals. The first two, who were unemployed, were the parents of the third, a minor who had suffered from disability since birth and had been registered as 100% disabled by the county civil invalidity board. They complained that they had not received the financial aid provided for by regional statute 16 of 1986. They contended generally that, by refusing their disabled child effective medical and financial assistance, the state was violating her right to life and health.

The Court held that Article 2 could not be relied upon in this case because the application did not concern a violation of the child's right to life, but rather the "health care and assistance to be given to the parents". It also noted that the parents were receiving benefit on a permanent basis to cope with their child's disabilities and that "the scale of that benefit showed that Italy was already discharging its positive obligations".

Calvelli and Ciglio v. Italy, judgment of 17 January 2002 (applicability)[68]

The applicants in this case, whose new-born baby suffered from a respiratory and neurological syndrome and had died 10 days after birth, had taken proceedings against the obstetrician. The criminal court found him guilty of involuntary manslaughter on the grounds that he had done nothing about the risk of the baby's being asphyxiated during delivery and had not taken preventive measures during the pregnancy. The court nevertheless suspended the sentence and ordered that the conviction should not appear on the doctor's criminal record. The criminal proceedings against the doctor were eventually time barred as a consequence of procedural failings which had delayed the investigation and hearing of the case. The applicants argued before the ECHR that a ruling that prosecution of an offence of homicide was time barred for reasons related to the exces-

67. Application No. 39712/98.
68. Application No. 32967/96.

sive length of the proceedings could not be compatible with Article 2 (§43).

The Court pointed out that Article 2 of the Convention enjoined the state to take appropriate steps to safeguard the lives of those within its jurisdiction and it decided to apply this principle to the sphere of public health (§§48-49). Nevertheless, because the applicants had agreed to a settlement with the insurers representing the doctor and the clinic, the Court concluded that they could no longer claim to be victims and that it was therefore not required to examine the case in the light of Article 2.

Nitecki v. Poland, decision of 21 March 2002 (inadmissible)[69]

The applicant, who had a life-threatening illness, had been prescribed a very expensive drug, 70% of the cost of which was refunded by the national insurance fund. He applied to the local fund, local social services and the Ministry of Health and Social Security for a full refund on the ground that he could not afford to pay the remaining 30%. The authorities rejected his request. The applicant complained before the Court that the refusal to refund the full price of the drug breached his right to life guaranteed by Article 2 of the Convention.

The Court said that "it cannot be excluded that the acts and omissions of the authorities in the field of health-care policy may in certain circumstances engage their responsibility under Article 2". It asserted that "with respect to the scope of the state's positive obligations in the provision of health care, ... an issue may arise under Article 2 where it is shown that the authorities of a contracting state put an individual's life at risk through the denial of health care which they have undertaken to make available to the population generally". In this case, the Court noted that the applicant's social security contributions made him eligible for health care by the public service. The Court concluded that "bearing in mind the medical treatment and facilities provided to the applicant, including a refund of the greater part of the cost of the required drug, the respondent state cannot be said, in the special circumstances of the present case, to have

69. Application No. 65653/01.

failed to discharge its obligations under Article 2 by not paying the remaining 30% of the drug price".

Article 3 (Prohibition of torture and inhuman or degrading treatment)

"No one shall be subjected to torture or to inhuman or degrading treatment or punishment."

Introduction

Article 3, like Article 2, embodies a fundamental value of democratic societies. It also places positive duties on states that have ratified the Convention to prevent the types of treatment in question.

In the above-mentioned case of *Larioshina v. Russia*,[70] the Court initiated a new approach to the protection of social rights by asserting that "a complaint about a wholly insufficient amount of social benefits may, in principle, raise an issue under Article 3 of the Convention, which prohibits inhuman or degrading treatment". In the case in question, however, there was no indication that the amount of the applicant's social benefits had caused such damage to her physical or mental health that it had attained the minimum level of severity to fall within the ambit of Article 3 of the Convention.

Examples of applying Article 3

Medical treatment

D v. the United Kingdom, judgment of 2 May 1997 (violation)[71]

The applicant, born in St Kitts (in the Caribbean), had been arrested on arrival in the United Kingdom for possessing cocaine and sentenced to six years' imprisonment. While he was serving his sentence he contracted pneumonia and was diagnosed with Aids. Before his release on parole, at an advanced stage of the illness, directions were given for his removal to St Kitts. Before the Court, he argued that his expulsion to St Kitts would condemn him to spend his remaining days in isolation and destitution,

70. See p. 27.

71. Case No. 146/1996/767/964.

with neither accommodation nor resources. The termination of the medical treatment he was receiving would hasten his death since no similar medical treatment was available in St Kitts.

The Court noted the gravity of the offence that had been committed by the applicant and expressed the view that imposing severe penalties, including expulsion, on persons involved in drug trafficking was a justified response to the scourge which trafficking represented (§46). However, in exercising its right to expel an individual to a third country, the contracting state must have regard to Article 3 of the Convention, which absolutely prohibited torture or inhuman or degrading treatment or punishment, and to the fact that its guarantees applied irrespective of the reprehensible nature of the conduct of the person in question (§47). Having thoroughly examined all the circumstances of the case, the Court noted that there was a serious risk that the unfavourable conditions in St Kitts would reduce the applicant's life expectancy and cause him extreme physical and psychological suffering.

The Court emphasised that aliens who had served prison sentences and were subject to expulsion could not in principle claim any entitlement to remain in the territory of a contracting state in order to continue to benefit from medical, social or other forms of assistance provided by the expelling state during their stay in prison. Nonetheless, "in the very exceptional circumstances of this case and given the compelling humanitarian considerations", it concluded that "executing the decision to expel the applicant would violate Article 3" (§54).

N.A.D.C. v. Switzerland, decision of 30 October 1998 (inadmissible)[72]

The applicant, an Angolan national, who had diabetes, had lodged an application for asylum immediately after his arrival in Switzerland. The Swiss authorities had dismissed his application on several grounds, the main one being that his state of health was not an obstacle to his being returned to Angola. Before the Commission, the applicant complained that sending him back to his country of origin was contrary to Articles 2

72. Application No. 46553/99.

and 3 of the Convention. He claimed that, owing to lack of financial resources, he would be unable to buy the medicine he needed and that this would lead ultimately to his death.

The Commission noted that, prior to his arrival in Switzerland, the applicant had received medical treatment in his country of origin and also pointed out that it would not be impossible for him to receive further treatment when he returned to Angola since the Swiss authorities had undertaken to give him financial assistance to cover his medical expenses for a specific length of time and a sum of money to allow him to resettle in Angola. It held that "the very exceptional circumstances and the compelling humanitarian considerations" at stake in *D v. the United Kingdom* had not been established in this case.

S.C.C. v. Sweden, decision of 15 February 2000 (inadmissible)[73]

The applicant had been refused a work permit and the Swedish immigration authorities had ordered that she be deported. A victim of Aids, she argued that she wished to undergo treatment in Sweden and cited humanitarian reasons in support of her application. She argued before the Court that her state of health would deteriorate radically if she was sent back to Zambia because the medical care she required was not available in her country.

The Court reiterated the principle that foreigners may not claim the right to remain in the territory of states solely to continue to undergo medical treatment. In exceptional circumstances, however, putting a deportation order into effect might violate Article 3 of the Convention where there were decisive humanitarian considerations. In this case, because medical treatment for Aids was provided in Zambia and the applicant's entire family was already in that country, the application was ruled manifestly unfounded and inadmissible.

73. Application No. 9384/81.

Free medical assistance or financial aid from the state

Pancenko v. Latvia, decision of 28 October 1999 (inadmissible)[74]

The applicant in this case, who had accumulated debts for municipal charges, complained of the hardship of her economic and social situation in Latvia, the fact of being unemployed and the lack of free medical treatment or financial support from the state.

The Court made it clear that the Convention did not guarantee economic and social rights as such, notably the right to work and the right to free medical assistance or financial support from the state to maintain a certain standard of living. At the same time, it accepted that a person's living conditions could fall within the scope of Article 3 of the Convention if they had attained a minimum level of severity. The Court ruled that the complaints advanced did not amount to a violation of the Convention.

Social services

Z and others v. the United Kingdom, judgment of 10 May 2001 (violation)[75]

This case concerned the degrading conditions in which the four applicants – who were minors – had been brought up and the ill-treatment inflicted on them by their parents. The applicants' family had been referred to the social services in 1987. From that date until they were placed in emergency care the children lived in filthy conditions, were malnourished and poorly socialised and showed signs of psychological disturbance. The child psychiatrist who examined them stated that "it was the worst case of neglect and emotional abuse" that she had encountered in her career (§40). Before the Court, the children's representatives alleged that the local authorities had not taken adequate steps to protect them from the severe negligence and abuse they had suffered and that this constituted a violation of Article 3.

The Court considered that the neglect and abuse suffered by the four children attained the level of severity to be qualified as inhuman and degrading treatment, and concluded that there had been a violation of

74. Application No. 40772/98.
75. Application No. 29392/95.

Article 3 of the Convention. The social services, being aware of the situation, had a positive obligation to protect the children. There was no doubt as to "the failure of the system to protect these applicant children from serious long-term neglect and abuse".

Article 8 (Right to respect for private and family life)

"1. Everyone has the right to respect for his private and family life, his home and his correspondence.

2. There shall be no interference by a public authority with the exercise of this right except such as is in accordance with the law and is necessary in a democratic society in the interests of national security, public safety or the economic well-being of the country, for the prevention of disorder or crime, for the protection of health or morals, or for the protection of the rights and freedoms of others."

Introduction

The main purpose of Article 8 is to safeguard individuals against arbitrary interference by public authorities. At the same time, it may create positive obligations for the state which are inherent in ensuring effective "respect" for private and family life.

Because the concept of "respect" is not precisely defined, states also enjoy a large measure of discretion as to how to meet their obligations in practice.

Examples of applying Article 8

Jitka Zehnalová and Otto Zehnal v. the Czech Republic, decision of 14 May 2002 (inadmissible)[76]

The applicants in this case were a woman with a physical disability and her husband. In contravention of national legislation, a large number of public buildings and buildings open to the public in the applicants' home town were not equipped with access facilities for people with impaired mobility. The applicants had applied to the administrative authorities and then to the courts to have the situation remedied but no decision had

76. Application No. 38621/97.

been taken. On the basis that Mrs Zehnalová was unable to enjoy a normal life, the applicants claimed there had been a violation of their right to respect for private life, under Article 8 of the Convention, and a further violation, on the same grounds, of Articles 12 and 13 of the European Social Charter.

While acknowledging that the state might have positive obligations under Article 8, the Court asserted that there had to be a direct link between the measures the state was urged to take and the applicant's private life. In this case, the Court took the view that the first applicant "[had] not demonstrated the existence of a special link between the lack of access to the buildings in question and the particular needs of her private life". It was doubtful whether the first applicant needed to use on a daily basis the large number of buildings complained of. The Court therefore considered that Article 8 was not applicable in the case.

Roche v. the United Kingdom [GC], judgment of 19 October 2005 (violation)[77]

The applicant claimed that his health problems were the result of his participation in tests of mustard gas and a nerve gas under the direction of the British armed forces at Porton Down. He applied for a service pension but his application was rejected on the ground that he could not demonstrate a causal link between the tests and the health problems. He unsuccessfully attempted to access official information that would have enabled the Pensions Appeal Tribunal to decide whether his condition had been caused or aggravated by his participation in the tests at Porton Down. He complained that he had been denied adequate access to the relevant information, in breach of Articles 8 and 10 of the Convention.

The chamber to which the case was assigned decided to relinquish jurisdiction to the Grand Chamber, which subsequently concluded that, while Article 1 of Protocol No. 1 and Articles 6§1 and 14 of the Convention were inapplicable, there had been a violation of Article 8.

The Court held that the long period of uncertainty as to whether or not he had been put at risk through his participation in the tests had

77. Application No. 32555/96.

caused Mr Roche anxiety and stress. The United Kingdom had not fulfilled "the positive obligation to provide an effective and accessible procedure enabling the applicant to have access to all relevant and appropriate information which would allow him to assess any risk to which he had been exposed".

Reference to the European Social Charter in the case-law of the European Court of Human Rights

Jazvinsky v. Slovakia, decision of 7 September 2000 (partially inadmissible)[78]

The applicant complained that he and his family had been mistreated, discriminated against and outright persecuted by the Slovakian authorities in various respects, notably in the rejection of an application for medical care and social benefit for his daughter, who was completely unable to walk. The applicant claimed that the state had failed to uphold the rights to work, social security and health protection and that the authorities, through their failure to provide appropriate assistance, had violated the principle of respect for human dignity. He alleged violations of Articles 3, 6§1, 8, 11, 13 and 14 of the Convention and Article 1 of the European Social Charter.

The Court stated that "the Convention does not guarantee, as such, the right to work, to social security or to protection of a person's health. These complaints are therefore incompatible *ratione materiae* with the Convention" (§7).

Jitka Zehnalová and Otto Zehnal v. the Czech Republic, decision of 14 May 2002 (inadmissible)[79]

The applicants in this case invoked Articles 12 and 13 of the European Social Charter.

The Court found that their allegations disclosed no appearance of a violation of the rights and freedoms guaranteed by the Convention and its Protocols. It also pointed out that it was not its task to review govern-

78. Applications Nos. 33088/96, 52236/99, 52451/99-52453/99, 52455/99 and 52457/99-52459/99.

79. Application No. 38621/97.

ments' compliance with instruments other than the European Convention on Human Rights and its Protocols, even if, like other international treaties, the European Social Charter might provide it with a source of inspiration.

The complaint was found to be incompatible *ratione materiae* with the Convention.

Execution of European Court of Human Rights judgments

Enforcement of the Court's judgments is the logical next step in the system of supranational legal protection to which the contracting states have committed themselves. Without a duty of enforcement the Court's judgments would be ineffectual.

States' obligation to comply with ECHR judgments

Under Article 46§1 of the Convention, the contracting states "undertake to abide by the final judgment of the Court in any case to which they are parties". Article 46§2 provides that the final judgment of the Court is to be "transmitted to the Committee of Ministers, which shall supervise its execution".

This undertaking entails very specific legal obligations, which are evident in Committee of Ministers practice under Article 46 (or formerly under Articles 32 and 54) and in the Court's case-law (see, below, *Substance of the obligation to execute judgments*, p. 49).

The system of protection established by the Convention thus includes machinery for collective supervision by the states' representatives, meeting in the Committee of Ministers. This arrangement, which ensures that respondent states accept the full implications of ECHR judgments,[80 81] is a practical and effective safeguard of Convention rights and freedoms.

SUBSTANCE OF THE OBLIGATION TO EXECUTE JUDGMENTS

In accordance with the system of responsibility under international law,[82] states have three obligations: to put an end to the specific illegality that infringed the Convention; to repair, as far as possible, its consequences (*restitutio in integrum*); and to avert further infringements.

These obligations are spelled out in the Court's case-law: "... a judgment in which the Court finds a breach imposes on the respondent state a legal obligation to put an end to the breach and make reparation for its consequences in such a way as to restore as far as possible the situation existing before the breach".[83]

This means that "the respondent state [has] a legal obligation not just to pay those concerned the sums awarded by way of just satisfaction, but also to choose, subject to supervision by the Committee of Ministers, the general and/or, if appropriate, individual measures to be adopted in [its] domestic legal order to put an end to the violation found by the Court".[84]

The obligations are also stated in interim resolutions of the Committee of Ministers[85] and, in particular, in a set of rules for applying Article 46§2 of

80. Including those in which the Court notes that a case has been settled amicably, where the respondent state undertakes to adopt individual measures in favour of the applicant or measures of a general nature.
81. In accordance with former Articles 32 and 54 of the Convention and with practice based on those articles, the same applied in respect of decisions by the Convention bodies before the entry into force of Protocol No. 11.
82. Based on acceptance of Article 1 of the Convention.
83. *Papamichalopoulos and Others v. Greece*, 31 October 1995, §§34 *et seq.*
84. *Scozzari and Giunta v. Italy*, 13 July 2000, Applications Nos 39221/98 and 41963/98, §249.
85. For example, in a resolution taking stock of measures adopted by Italy following numerous infringements of the right to a hearing within a reasonable time, the Committee stressed "the necessity for all contracting states to take rapidly all the measures required in order to ... prevent new violations of the Convention similar to those found" (Resolution DH (97) 336). In a resolution taking stock of measures adopted by Greece following violations concerning failure to enforce domestic court rulings, the Committee noted in relation to one case that "the consequences of the violation found were completely erased" and that in relation to other cases "the violations found by the European Court only resulted in pecuniary losses which were fully compensated through payment of compensation awarded either by the domestic authorities or by the European Court under Article 41 of the Convention. No. further individual measures were thus required" (*Hornsby v. Greece* and other cases, ResDH (2004) 81).

the Convention which the Ministers' Deputies adopted at their 736th meeting, on 10 January 2001.[86]

Enforcing judgments of the Court implies a duty to deliver three things: just satisfaction, individual measures and general measures.

The Court orders payment of just satisfaction, as appropriate, under Article 41 of the Convention. This normally takes the form of a sum of money to make good pecuniary and non-pecuniary damage and to cover costs. Interest for late payment is added to the sum after expiry of a time limit fixed by the Court. The just-satisfaction award is detailed in the judgment and is directly enforceable. For example, in the case of *Roche v. the United Kingdom*, in which it found there had been a violation of Article 8, the Court awarded the applicant €8 000 for non-pecuniary damage and €47 000 in costs.

Because just satisfaction does not always repair the consequences of a violation adequately, execution of a judgment may also necessitate individual measures in favour of the applicant. These could include reopening proceedings found to be unfair; not enforcing a national measure or domestic decision or cancelling it; or adopting new provisions – e.g. for speedy execution of a domestic court decision whose non-execution had contravened the Convention, or to speed up proceedings still ongoing when the Court delivered its judgment. In the case of *Schuler-Zgraggen v. Switzerland*, for example (see above, p. 35), the Court found that proceedings concerning social security benefit had been unfair on account of sex discrimination. After the ECHR judgment the contested proceedings were

86. See document CM (2000) 185, Appendix 3.
Rule 3b. [...] the Committee of Ministers shall examine whether:
- any just satisfaction awarded by the Court has been paid, including, as the case may be, default interest; and, if required, and taking into account the discretion of the state concerned to choose the means necessary to comply with the judgment, whether:
- individual measures have been taken to ensure that the violation has ceased and that the injured party is put, as far as possible, in the same situation as that party enjoyed prior to the violation of the Convention;
- general measures have been adopted preventing new violations similar to that or those found, or putting an end to continuing violations.

reopened and the applicant was retrospectively awarded the benefits she had claimed.

In certain cases, enforcement of a judgment may require general measures to prevent new breaches of the Convention. The measures may take the form of changes to judicial practice, laws or regulations; translation and circulation of the judgment at national level; or practical measures such as setting up a court, building a prison, recruiting judges or providing police training. For example, in *Kovachev v. Bulgaria* (see above, p. 12) – which concerned unfairness of judicial proceedings, the applicant having been unable to take his welfare-benefit claim to an independent and impartial tribunal – Bulgaria acted on the violation finding by introducing legislative and regulatory measures which made a legal remedy available to anyone in a similar situation.

FREEDOM OF CHOICE FOR THE RESPONDENT STATE AND SUPERVISION BY THE COMMITTEE OF MINISTERS

If a Court judgment declares that the Convention has been violated, the state concerned has a large measure of freedom with regard to rectifying the applicant's situation and preventing new violations. That freedom is always closely contingent, however, on supervision by the Committee of Ministers and proper execution of the judgment.

The Court has made the point that, "subject to monitoring by the Committee of Ministers, the respondent state remains free to choose the means by which it will discharge its legal obligation under Article 46 of the Convention, provided that such means are compatible with the conclusions set out in the Court's judgment".[87]

Apart from pecuniary compensation, the Court does not, as a rule, specify individual or general measures to be adopted.

Nonetheless, it has on occasion restricted the choice of means of execution. In certain cases where an applicant had been deprived of property,

87. Judgment in *Scozzari and Giunta v. Italy*, 13 July 2000, Applications Nos. 39221/98 and 41963/98.

it has ruled that the state should either return the property or, failing that, pay certain sums of money to the applicant.[88] The Court went one step further in its judgment of 8 April 2004 in *Assanidzé v. Georgia.*[89] It stipulated in the judgment that the respondent state must release the applicant from custody at the earliest possible date because "by its very nature, the violation found in the instant case does not leave any real choice as to the measures required to remedy it".

To ensure the effectiveness of the Convention supervisory system, the Council of Europe Committee of Ministers adopted a resolution on 12 May 2004 (Res (2004) 3) on judgments which reveal an underlying systemic problem, and a recommendation on the same date (Rec (2004) 6) on the improvement of domestic remedies.

In the resolution the Committee of Ministers asks the Court to identify in its judgments any underlying systemic problem and the source of the problem.[90] In Recommendation Rec (2004) 6, it makes the point that improvement of domestic remedies, particularly in repeat cases, should help to reduce the Court's workload.

Referring to these documents, the Court has indicated, for example in its judgment in *Broniowski v. Poland*[91] on 22 June 2004, the type of general measures that a country should take in order to prevent a large number of similar cases coming before it.

EXECUTION PROCEDURE

The final judgment of the Court is sent to the Committee of Ministers and the respondent state is required to notify the Committee of measures taken for its execution.

The information that the state supplies is examined, at special Human Rights ("DH/HR") meetings, in the light of the *Rules adopted by the Com-*

88. See the judgments in *Papamichalopoulos and others v. Greece* (Article 50), 31 October 1995, and *Brumărescu v. Romania* (just satisfaction).
89. Application No. 71503/01.
90. Paragraph I of the resolution.
91. Application No. 31443/96.

mittee of Ministers for the application of Article 46, paragraph 2, of the European Convention on Human Rights.[92] The agendas of these meetings are published. At each DH/HR meeting the Committee of Ministers considers information about the payment of just satisfaction awarded by the Court or the adoption of individual measures. General measures are supervised on a six-monthly basis unless the Committee decides otherwise.[93]

The Council of Europe's Directorate General of Human Rights and Legal Affairs has a department dealing with execution of ECHR judgments which assists the Committee of Ministers in its supervisory function. The Committee, in close cooperation with the authorities of the state concerned, decides what measures need to be taken to comply with the Court judgment.

To facilitate execution of the judgment, the Committee may, during its examination of the case, adopt interim resolutions. These may contain information concerning interim measures already taken and set a provisional timetable for the reforms; encourage the respondent state to pursue certain reforms; or insist that it take the measures needed to comply with the judgment. In the event of failure to execute a judgment, the Committee of Ministers may exert political or diplomatic pressure or may adopt more incisive interim resolutions[94] to ensure that the state complies. In practice, that is very rarely needed because a satisfactory solution can almost always be found through constructive dialogue.

Not until the Committee has established that the judgment has been complied with does it adopt a resolution saying that the state has fulfilled its obligations under Article 46§2 of the Convention. Until the state has

92. Text approved by the Committee of Ministers on 10 January 2001 at the 736th meeting of the Ministers' Deputies.
93. See Rule 4, "Control intervals".
94. See, in particular, Interim Resolution ResDH (2000) 105 concerning the judgment of the European Court of Human Rights of 28 July 1998 in the case of *Loizidou v. Turkey*, in which the Committee of Ministers asserted that "the refusal of Turkey to execute the judgment of the Court demonstrates a manifest disregard for its international obligations, both as a High Contracting Party to the Convention and as a member state of the Council of Europe" and insisted "in view of the gravity of the matter … that Turkey comply fully and without any further delay with the European Court of Human Rights judgment of 28 July 1998".

taken satisfactory measures, explanations, justification or action will continue to be required of it and no final resolution will be adopted.

The entry into force of Protocol No. 14 will introduce certain changes in the system for the execution of judgments.[95]

95. For more information see Elisabeth Lambert-Abdelgawad, "Le Protocole 14 et l'exécution des arrêts de la Cour européenne des Droits de l'Homme", in *Droit et Justice* 61 (*La réforme du système contentieux de la Convention européenne des Droits de l'Homme*), Nemesis, Bruylant, 2005, pp. 79-113.

Examples of execution measures adopted by states in the social security field[96]

Procedural safeguards (Article 6§1)

Access to an independent and impartial tribunal

In the case of *Kovachev v. Bulgaria*[97] the Commission decided there had been a violation of Article 6§1 of the Convention on account of the applicant's not having access to an independent and impartial tribunal for determination of his right to certain welfare allowances. The denial of access had resulted from application of the 1992 Social Welfare Regulations, which made no provision for appeal to the courts concerning social benefits and assigned sole jurisdiction in the matter to the administrative authorities.

To prevent further such violations, Bulgaria amended its Social Welfare Act and the relevant implementing regulations, which now provide for appeal to the courts against decisions of regional social welfare departments (see Resolution ResDH (2001) 3, adopted by the Committee of Ministers on 26 February 2001).

96. *The execution of the European Court of Human Rights' judgments in the field of social security,* S. Günter Nagel, *Revue de droit sanitaire et sociale*, n° 2, pp. 204-215, Paris 2007.

97. Application No. 29303/95.

In its judgment of 28 June 2005 in *Zedník v. the Czech Republic*[98] – concerning the Czech authorities' withdrawal of the applicant's partial invalidity allowance – the ECHR held that the Czech Constitutional Court's interpretation of a procedural requirement had prevented examination of the merits of the applicant's case and so had infringed the right to effective protection by the courts.

Following the judgment, the Czech Republic reviewed its legislation and judicial practice in order to clarify the admissibility requirements for appeals to the Constitutional Court, and specifically the rules on time limits for lodging appeals and on exhaustion of domestic remedies.

However, this did not solve the problem of the Constitutional Court's over-insistence on procedural formalities in ruling certain cases to be inadmissible, as in *Zedník* and *Kadlec and Bulena*.[99] At the Committee of Ministers' invitation, the Constitutional Court discussed the matter at one of its plenary assemblies. To avert fresh violations, the Committee of Ministers then suggested publishing the conclusions of this discussion as a press release. The relevant ECHR judgments were also translated into Czech, published on the Ministry of Justice website and circulated to the authorities concerned.[100]

Length of proceedings

The cases of *Deumeland v. the Federal Republic of Germany* and *Beumer v. the Netherlands* confirmed the need for procedural expeditiousness in social-security matters. It is usual in cases of this type for the Committee of Ministers to request that proceedings pending in national courts be speeded up and it may even expect them to be concluded before it closes it examination of the case. It will ask for judgments be published and circulated to the relevant domestic authorities so that they can take account of the Court's judgments.[101]

98. Application No. 74328/01.
99. Judgments of 20 April 2004 and 25 May 2004; see Annotated Agenda of the 948th (DH) meeting of the Ministers' Deputies, 29-30 November 2005, CM/Del/OJ/DH (2005) 948, Vol. I.
100. See Annotated Agenda of the 966th (DH) meeting of the Ministers' Deputies, 6 June 2006, CM/Del/OJ/DH (2006) 966, Vol. I.

Failure to execute a judgment or administrative decision

In the case of *Burdov v. Russia* the ECHR concluded that Article 6§1 of the Convention and Article 1 of Protocol No. 1 had been contravened by several years' non-execution by the Russian welfare authorities of final court decisions ordering them to pay the applicant various compensation and allowances (with subsequent indexing) for health damage sustained in emergency operations at the Chernobyl nuclear plant.

The judgment had a range of consequences. To prevent further infringements, the Russian Government had to pay people in situations similar to that of the applicant the arrears accumulated as a result of the non-execution of domestic judgments. This involved executing more than 5 000 other domestic decisions on indexing of allowances to victims of the Chernobyl disaster. The Government allocated the social-security authorities the necessary resources to meet their financial obligations arising from similar judgments. In addition, on 2 April 2004, the Russian Parliament amended the legislation on social insurance of Chernobyl victims. The new law, which has been in force since 29 April 2004, provides for a new system of index-linked allowances based on the inflation rate used to calculate the next year's federal budget.[102]

Allowances for Chernobyl victims are just one of the areas in which the Committee of Ministers, in cooperation with the Russian authorities, has sought solutions to non-execution of court decisions. The ECHR has also delivered a number of similar judgments – in *Makarova and others v. Russia*, for example – in this same sphere of social security.[103] The *Makarova* case concerned failure to enforce a court order that the amount of pension paid to the applicants by the social welfare office be increased.

---

101. See Annotated Agenda of the 966th (DH) meeting of the Ministers' Deputies, 6 June 2006, CM/Del/OJ/DH (2006) 966, Vol. I, case of *Mocie v. France*.
102. See Resolution ResDH (2004) 85 adopted by the Committee of Ministers on 22 December 2004.
103. Judgment of 24 February 2005, Application No. 7023/03

PROHIBITION OF DISCRIMINATION (ARTICLE 14)

In the wake of certain Court judgments a number of member states have amended their social-security provisions in order to eliminate discrimination, notably on the grounds of sex and nationality.

Discrimination on the ground of sex

The Court concluded in the case of *Schuler-Zgraggen v. Switzerland* that there had been a violation of Article 14 of the Convention in conjunction with Article 6§1. It held that it had been discriminatory to withdraw the applicant's invalidity benefit on the birth of her son on the ground that she coped with household and child and was therefore capable of working.

Following the Court's judgment, the Swiss authorities decided to reopen the contested proceedings. After a fresh hearing the Federal Insurance Court awarded the applicant full invalidity benefit with arrears.[104]

In the case of *Wessels-Bergervoet v. the Netherlands*[105] the Court found that the reduction of the applicant's old-age pension constituted unjustified discrimination.

The relevant legislation in the Netherlands was amended in April 1985 – before the ECHR judgment had actually been delivered – to give married women the right to an independent old-age pension. After the Court's judgment, however, in order to remove the discriminatory effects of the former provisions, the law was further amended retroactively as of 1 January 2002. All married or previously married women whose husbands or former husbands worked without full insurance before 1985 were now entitled to full old-age pension. In addition, all women who had been on reduced pension before 1 January 2002 and had taken legal action to contest the reduction received full pension as from the date of their pension award. Women who had taken no legal action were not compensated automatically but drew full pension as from 1 January 2002.[106]

104. See Resolution DH (95) 95, adopted by the Committee of Ministers on 7 June 1995.
105. Judgment of 4 June 2002, Application No. 34462/97.
106. See Resolution ResDH (2005) 91, adopted by the Committee of Ministers on 26 October 2005.

The Court also concluded that there had been discrimination contrary to the Convention in *Willis v. the United Kingdom*, which had to do with certain social benefits for widowed parents being payable to women and not men.

The United Kingdom Government took measures to prevent fresh infringements of the same type by passing the Welfare Reform and Pensions Act 1999, sections 54 and 55 of which put widowers and widows on an equal footing with regard to social benefits from 9 April 2001.[107]

In its judgment in *Van Raalte v. the Netherlands*, the Court condemned the situation that existed in the Netherlands before 1989, when, under the General Child Care Benefits Act, unmarried, childless men aged 45 and over were required to pay contributions to the family benefit scheme whereas women in the same circumstances were exempt. The authorities in the Netherlands rescinded the disputed provision. As of 1 January 1989, men and women were required to pay the same contributions, irrespective of age, marital status and whether or not they had children (see §28 of the ECHR judgment).

Discrimination on the ground of nationality

In the case of *Gaygusuz v. Austria*, the Court concluded that Article 14 had been contravened by the Austrian authorities' refusal to award the applicant – who was long-term unemployed and had lost the right to unemployment benefit – an advance on his pension in the form of an "emergency allowance" on the ground that he was not of Austrian nationality.

Following the judgment, the Austrian Parliament amended Articles 33 and 34 of the 1977 Unemployment Insurance Act (*Arbeitslosenversicherungsgesetz*) and stopped making Austrian nationality a condition of entitlement to emergency assistance.[108]

A violation of Article 14 was also found in the case of *Koua Poirrez v. France*, in which the applicant had been refused an allowance for disabled

107. See Resolution ResDH (2003) 130, adopted by the Committee of Ministers on 22 July 2003.
108. See Resolution DH (98) 372 adopted by the Committee of Ministers on 12 November 1998.

adults – on the ground that he was not a French national – although he resided in France, was the adopted son of a French citizen and had been officially registered as a disabled person.

The French authorities repealed the discriminatory provision in 1998 and the applicant was able to obtain the allowance for which he had applied. The ECHR also awarded him a total of €20 000 in just satisfaction for pecuniary and non-pecuniary damage. The Committee of Ministers noted these measures.[109]

The Court's case-law has provided a model for domestic courts. In France, for example, in the case of *Bozkurt v. CPAM de Saint-Etienne*[110] the Court of Cassation ruled that a refusal to award a supplementary allowance from the National Solidarity Fund on the ground that the applicant was of Turkish nationality violated Article 14 of the Convention and Article 1 of Protocol No. 1. In basing its judgment on the right to non-discrimination in combination with the right to enjoyment of property, the Court of Cassation's Social Division drew directly on the ECHR findings in *Gaygusuz v. Austria*.

Discrimination in relation to other categories of people

Also held to be discriminatory, in *Buche v. the Czech Republic*,[111] was suspension of a former military judge's army pension under 1993 legislation.

Following the ECHR judgment, the Czech authorities notified the Committee of Ministers that the Ministry of Defence had decided to resume paying pension to the applicant and the (dozen) other people in the same situation.[112] On the basis of this information, after deciding that it is satis-

109. See Annotated Agenda of the 879th (DH) meeting of the Ministers' Deputies, 5 and 6 April 2004, CM/Del/OJ/OT (2004) 879.

110. Court of Cassation, Social Division, judgment of 14 January 1999, JCP, 1999, II, 10082, note F. Sudre.

111. Judgment of 26 November 2002, Application No. 36541/97.

112. See Annotated Agenda of the 871st (DH) meeting of the Ministers' Deputies, 10 and 11 February 2004, CM/Del/OJ/OT (2004) 871.

factory, the Committee of Ministers will adopt a final resolution concluding its examination of execution of the judgment.

Protection of property (Article 1 of Protocol No. 1)

In the case of *Kjartan Ásmundsson v. Iceland*, the ECHR concluded that the applicant's right to the enjoyment of his property had been breached. Application of new legislation on invalidity pensions had resulted in total cessation of an invalidity pension which he had been receiving.

Under Article 41[113] of the Convention, the Court awarded Mr Ásmundsson €75 000 for the pecuniary damage resulting from the termination of his invalidity pension. However, it did not award him the full amount he had claimed as the new rules had been prompted by legitimate concerns and were based on objective criteria. To prevent further violations, the Committee of Ministers, in co-operation with the Icelandic authorities, examined general measures including payment of compensation to other people in situations similar to the applicant's.[114]

In its judgment of 12 July 2005 in *Solodyuk v. Russia,*[115] the Court concluded that the applicants' right to the enjoyment of their property (under Article 1 of Protocol No. 1) had been infringed by delayed payment of their old-age pension (in 1998) and depreciation of the pension due.[116]

The consequences of the violation were made good by an award of just satisfaction, and no further individual measures were required. To prevent fresh violations, the Committee of Ministers asked the Russian authorities to notify it of measures taken or envisaged to prevent delays in pension payments and to ensure that pensions held their value. It also

113. Article 41 – Just satisfaction: "If the Court finds that there has been a violation of the Convention or the protocols thereto, and if the internal law of the High Contracting Party concerned allows only partial reparation to be made, the Court shall, if necessary, afford just satisfaction to the injured party."

114. See Annotated Agenda of the 928th meeting (DH) of the Ministers' Deputies, 6 and 7 June 2005, CM/Del/OJ/DH (2005) 928, Vol. II.

115. Application No. 67099/01.

116. As a result of the difference between the rate of indexation for pensions and the inflation rate in Russia at the time, which had reached 37%.

asked for the Court's judgment to be published and insisted that it be communicated to both the Ministry of Labour and the pension fund.

Conclusion

There has been considerable evolution in recent years in the Court's case-law concerning social security, with a marked trend towards more extensive protection of rights despite the significant margin of discretion which the Convention allows in relation to states' pecuniary obligations.

The interpretation given to the concept of "civil rights and obligations" has made it possible to apply the Article 6§1 procedural guarantees to both social benefits and social contributions. In addition, the judges in Strasbourg have placed particular emphasis on the requirement that national authorities should act promptly in cases concerning social security, especially health care, benefit following work accidents, invalidity allowances and emergency welfare support.

Alongside the procedural safeguards, substantive protection of rights has also developed and strengthened. Broad interpretation of the concepts of possessions and of claims against the state has extended the applicability of Article 1 of Protocol No. 1 (Protection of property) to many cases in the social security sphere.

Contributory benefits were the first to be accepted as falling within the Commission's and Court's definition of possessions. The concept was later extended to embrace non-contributory benefits and social assistance provided for by statute.

These rights, moreover, may derive not only from national legislation but also from international law.

The Grand Chamber judgment in the case of *Stec and others v. the United Kingdom* in 2006 confirmed this breadth of interpretation and included interests within the concept of "possessions". In ruling this case to be admissible, the Court stated that if a social security benefit (whether contributory or non contributory) is provided for under national law, it created a "proprietary interest" falling within the ambit of Article 1 of Protocol No. 1.

This judgment was regarded in some quarters[117] as applying Protocol No. 12 to the Convention ahead of its actually coming into force. Protocol No. 12 prohibits discrimination in any form, so further extension of protection may be anticipated once it does come into force.

Articles 2, 3 and 8 of the Convention have opened new avenues of protection. As we have seen, all these articles can create positive obligations for the state with regard to the protection of life, the prohibition of torture and inhuman and degrading treatment, and respect for private and family life. In the case of *Calvelli and Ciglio v. Italy*, the Court confirmed that the principles of Article 2 of the Convention extended to the sphere of public health. This development may be seen as a means of affirming the right to protection of health laid down in Article 11 of the European Social Charter. It is necessary, however, to demonstrate the existence of a direct and immediate link between a state's positive obligations and the rights protected by these articles.

117. Such is the reasoning of, for example, the United Kingdom Government and Judge Borrego Borrego in his concurring opinion: "The applicants were seeking to widen the concept of a 'possession' to include claims which had no basis in domestic law, in order to bring a general complaint of discrimination of the type which would be covered by the new Protocol No. 12 but not by Article 14."

Appendix: list of the principal cases

Other titles in the "Human rights files" series

The position of aliens in relation to the European Convention on Human Rights 2nd ed. Hélène Lambert, *2007*

Freedom of expression in Europe: case-law concerning Article 10 of the European Convention on Human Rights. Directorate General of Human Rights, *2007*

Environmental protection and the European Convention on Human Rights. Daniel I. García San José, *2005*

Article 9 of the European Convention on Human Rights : freedom of thought, conscience and religion. Jean-François Renucci, *2005*

Introduction to the European Convention on Human Rights: the rights guaranteed and the protection mechanism. Jean-François Renucci, *2005*

Article 5 of the European Convention on Human Rights: the protection of liberty and security of person. Jim Murdoch, *2002*

The execution of judgments of the European Court of Human Rights. Elisabeth Lambert-Abdelgawad, *2002*

Asylum and the European Convention on Human Rights 3rd ed. Nuala Mole, *2000*

The margin of appreciation : interpretation and discretion under the European Convention on Human Rights. Steven Greer, *2000*

The European Convention on Human Rights and property rights rev. ed. Laurent Sermet, *1998*

The exceptions to Articles 8 to 11 of the European Convention on Human Rights. Steven Greer, *1997*

To order these titles and more, see Council of Europe Publishing on the Internet, http://book.coe.int/

Sales agents for publications of the Council of Europe
Agents de vente des publications du Conseil de l'Europe

BELGIUM/BELGIQUE
La Librairie Européenne -
The European Bookshop
Rue de l'Orme, 1
B-1040 BRUXELLES
Tel.: +32 (0)2 231 04 35
Fax: +32 (0)2 735 08 60
E-mail: order@libeurop.be
http://www.libeurop.be

Jean De Lannoy
Avenue du Roi 202 Koningslaan
B-1190 BRUXELLES
Tel.: +32 (0)2 538 43 08
Fax: +32 (0)2 538 08 41
E-mail: jean.de.lannoy@dl-servi.com
http://www.jean-de-lannoy.be

CANADA
Renouf Publishing Co. Ltd.
1-5369 Canotek Road
OTTAWA, Ontario K1J 9J3, Canada
Tel.: +1 613 745 2665
Fax: +1 613 745 7660
Toll-Free Tel.: (866) 767-6766
E-mail: order.dept@renoufbooks.com
http://www.renoufbooks.com

CZECH REPUBLIC/ RÉPUBLIQUE TCHÈQUE
Suweco CZ, s.r.o.
Klecakova 347
CZ-180 21 PRAHA 9
Tel.: +420 2 424 59 204
Fax: +420 2 848 21 646
E-mail: import@suweco.cz
http://www.suweco.cz

DENMARK/DANEMARK
GAD
Vimmelskaftet 32
DK-1161 KØBENHAVN K
Tel.: +45 77 66 60 00
Fax: +45 77 66 60 01
E-mail: gad@gad.dk
http://www.gad.dk

FINLAND/FINLANDE
Akateeminen Kirjakauppa
PO Box 128
Keskuskatu 1
FIN-00100 HELSINKI
Tel.: +358 (0)9 121 4430
Fax: +358 (0)9 121 4242
E-mail: akatilaus@akateeminen.com
http://www.akateeminen.com

FRANCE
La Documentation française
(diffusion/distribution France entière)
124, rue Henri Barbusse
F-93308 AUBERVILLIERS CEDEX
Tél.: +33 (0)1 40 15 70 00
Fax: +33 (0)1 40 15 68 00
E-mail: commande@ladocumentationfrancaise.fr
http://www.ladocumentationfrancaise.fr

Librairie Kléber
1 rue des Francs Bourgeois
F-67000 STRASBOURG
Tel.: +33 (0)3 88 15 78 88
Fax: +33 (0)3 88 15 78 80
E-mail: francois.wolfermann@librairie-kleber.fr
http://www.librairie-kleber.com

GERMANY/ALLEMAGNE AUSTRIA/AUTRICHE
UNO Verlag GmbH
August-Bebel-Allee 6
D-53175 BONN
Tel.: +49 (0)228 94 90 20
Fax: +49 (0)228 94 90 222
E-mail: bestellung@uno-verlag.de
http://www.uno-verlag.de

GREECE/GRÈCE
Librairie Kauffmann s.a.
Stadiou 28
GR-105 64 ATHINAI
Tel.: +30 210 32 55 321
Fax.: +30 210 32 30 320
E-mail: ord@otenet.gr
http://www.kauffmann.gr

HUNGARY/HONGRIE
Euro Info Service kft.
1137 Bp. Szent István krt. 12.
H-1137 BUDAPEST
Tel.: +36 (06)1 329 2170
Fax: +36 (06)1 349 2053
E-mail: euroinfo@euroinfo.hu
http://www.euroinfo.hu

ITALY/ITALIE
Licosa SpA
Via Duca di Calabria, 1/1
I-50125 FIRENZE
Tel.: +39 0556 483215
Fax: +39 0556 41257
E-mail: licosa@licosa.com
http://www.licosa.com

MEXICO/MEXIQUE
Mundi-Prensa México, S.A. De C.V.
Río Pánuco, 141 Delegacíon Cuauhtémoc
06500 MÉXICO, D.F.
Tel.: +52 (01)55 55 33 56 58
Fax: +52 (01)55 55 14 67 99
E-mail: mundiprensa@mundiprensa.com.mx
http://www.mundiprensa.com.mx

NETHERLANDS/PAYS-BAS
De Lindeboom Internationale Publicaties b.v.
M.A. de Ruyterstraat 20 A
NL-7482 BZ HAAKSBERGEN
Tel.: +31 (0)53 5740004
Fax: +31 (0)53 5729296
E-mail: books@delindeboom.com
http://www.delindeboom.com

NORWAY/NORVÈGE
Akademika
Postboks 84 Blindern
N-0314 OSLO
Tel.: +47 2 218 8100
Fax: +47 2 218 8103
E-mail: support@akademika.no
http://www.akademika.no

POLAND/POLOGNE
Ars Polona JSC
25 Obroncow Street
PL-03-933 WARSZAWA
Tel.: +48 (0)22 509 86 00
Fax: +48 (0)22 509 86 10
E-mail: arspolona@arspolona.com.pl
http://www.arspolona.com.pl

PORTUGAL
Livraria Portugal
(Dias & Andrade, Lda.)
Rua do Carmo, 70
P-1200-094 LISBOA
Tel.: +351 21 347 42 82 / 85
Fax: +351 21 347 02 64
E-mail: info@livrariaportugal.pt
http://www.livrariaportugal.pt

RUSSIAN FEDERATION/ FÉDÉRATION DE RUSSIE
Ves Mir
9a, Kolpacnhyi per.
RU-101000 MOSCOW
Tel.: +7 (8)495 623 6839
Fax: +7 (8)495 625 4269
E-mail: orders@vesmirbooks.ru
http://www.vesmirbooks.ru

SPAIN/ESPAGNE
Mundi-Prensa Libros, s.a.
Castelló, 37
E-28001 MADRID
Tel.: +34 914 36 37 00
Fax: +34 915 75 39 98
E-mail: libreria@mundiprensa.es
http://www.mundiprensa.com

SWITZERLAND/SUISSE
Van Diermen Editions – ADECO
Chemin du Lacuez 41
CH-1807 BLONAY
Tel.: +41 (0)21 943 26 73
Fax: +41 (0)21 943 36 05
E-mail: info@adeco.org
http://www.adeco.org

UNITED KINGDOM/ROYAUME-UNI
The Stationery Office Ltd
PO Box 29
GB-NORWICH NR3 1GN
Tel.: +44 (0)870 600 5522
Fax: +44 (0)870 600 5533
E-mail: book.enquiries@tso.co.uk
http://www.tsoshop.co.uk

UNITED STATES and CANADA/ ÉTATS-UNIS et CANADA
Manhattan Publishing Company
468 Albany Post Road
CROTTON-ON-HUDSON, NY 10520, USA
Tel.: +1 914 271 5194
Fax: +1 914 271 5856
E-mail: Info@manhattanpublishing.com
http://www.manhattanpublishing.com

Council of Europe Publishing/Editions du Conseil de l'Europe
F-67075 Strasbourg Cedex
Tel.: +33 (0)3 88 41 25 81 – Fax: +33 (0)3 88 41 39 10 – E-mail: publishing@coe.int – Website: http://book.coe.int